Dear Donna —

I hope you enjoy this book of poetry written by my mother.

With much love & appreciation,

Anna

HOLDING the SUN

HOLDING the SUN

poems

DEANNA MORGAN

MORGANSTAR MEDIA

Morganstar Media
Morgan Communications, Inc.
P.O. Box 101
Buhl, Idaho 83316
ISBN 978-0-692-87169-0

To Judy, who emboldened me,

to Rand, who makes actual my dreams,

and with grateful thanks to each of you

who at one time said, "I like that one."

Acknowledgements

I wish to express grateful appreciation to Ellen Tidwell, Claire Morgan, and Jane Alexander for their careful reading of the manuscript and for their insightful comments and corrections, and to Ladd Morgan for his perceptive suggestions. This book could never have been published without the tireless work, keen understanding, and wise suggestions of my husband, Randall. I am extremely grateful to so many friends who earnestly encouraged me to publish these poems.

DM

Contents

Strange and Divine Destinies

Lunch on the Ditch Bank

On the Way to My Grandfather's

Meditations From Tuttle

Further Acknowledgements

Preface

Commenting through poetry on this strange and splendid pilgrimage has been my way to puzzle, marvel, and share. Our journey isn't effortless. The lessons are demanding. But it is a profound privilege to take the journey and to know that we are deliberately watched over along the way, and that whatever paths we may have taken in the past, the path before us is unsullied.

My lessons began in a little town by a field of sugar beets when I came from God who is our home, as the poet said, and took my first breath of Earth's air. I grew up in Idaho, a descendent of Mormon pioneers, some who came west as refugees in the great Mormon exodus of 1847, and others who followed later from Sweden and Denmark. It is interesting that those we don't know often strongly inform whom we become.

I graduated from the University of California, Berkeley, married there and a few weeks later, my husband, Randall, and I left for Guatemala, a land riven by civil war, where we would be Peace Corps volunteers in an extremely remote Mayan village in the highlands. Like Thoreau's, our life was "driven into a corner and reduced to its lowest terms." It was there that I began to see life for what it is—a profound adventure. The poem *San Bartolomé Jocotenango* tells some of that story.

Home from Guatemala, I had the gentle experience of teaching English and world history in rural Idaho. My classroom was spacious and high upstairs in an old red brick schoolhouse with tall windows looking out across fields of beans and alfalfa. We had good horses and a good dog. *Summer Lunch* was written in those years.

We returned to California when Randall was a graduate student in the documentary film program at Stanford. We lived at Woodhaven in a little cottage hidden away in the redwood forest high above Palo Alto. It was here that I embarked on my supreme adventure–being a mother. *The Orchard* and *Mid–December in La Honda* come from that era.

We raised our seven children on a small ranch on the Snake River in Idaho. It was a life full of children, horses, cows, chickens, canoes, documentary films, and of Thousand Springs Academy, our century-old, one-room schoolhouse, where much of the children's education took place. Many of the poems in this collection evoke these times– *There Were Days of Golden Air, Morning on Chalk Hill, The Starling, Down at the River,* and others.

For many years in Idaho we were members of a Spanish-speaking Mormon congregation, and it seems that our family's life has always had something of an Hispanic accent. The children all grew up to serve missions for the Church in far-flung places. Later, Randall and I did, too, when we were missionaries in Gamu, a small village in the rice fields of the northern Philippines. *The Mission, Idaho Moon,* and *Salamat* grew out of that experience. The value of the mission, strong then, continues to unfold.

Over the years, our documentary film work has led us to interesting places and people. Currently, we also volunteer as media specialists in the Mormon humanitarian outreach to refugees and the homeless in the Bay Area. Through this experience, we have made good friends who teach us fundamental lessons, as reflected in *No One Left Behind* and *Wood Street CA*.

We divide our year between our home in the San Francisco Bay Area, our home on the Snake River in Idaho, and the places our film projects take us. Wherever we go, I am delighted by the diversity of peoples and cultures we encounter, yet I am struck by our profound alikeness. We are all crossing what the nineteenth century Mormon poet Eliza R. Snow calls "the boisterous ocean of circumstance." As my poem *The Story* suggests, our lives are "intricately woven from a single source" and "together we share this rough and smooth, sweet and sad, and ultimately triumphant story."

DeAnna Morgan

Lord God of fresh bread and tranquil mornings . . .

— Norman Corwin, *On a Note of Triumph*

Holding the Sun

High Desert, Deep Canyons

The Desert

Cheer my heart, old desert,
fill me with a sagebrush joy
and teach me the gratitude of morning.

Sweep me with desert rain
and comfort me with soft grass,
spring green.

Allow me to be one
with your resplendent spider webs
and your inimitable larks.

Strengthen me, friend,
and teach me your completeness.

Ketchum, Idaho

It was a good summer,
except for the range fires.
The sun was a bright orange ball
in the dead middle of day.
You could stare right at it.
It sat there naked and accessible
in the heavy gold air.

But Ketchum was cooler than the valley,
and the air clean.
The silent cemetery was green and peaceful
and Baby Alice in her blue seersucker dress
danced barefoot on the long, cool slab
over Hemingway's grave,
Papa's grave, beneath the two tall pines
casting long shadows toward the bald hills.

The world is burning
but the world is nothing to Papa
nor to his Mary, right next door.
And Hemingway is nothing to Alice
but the coolness of the marble on her feet.

Life is not what we think.
It's not the burning
nor the dying
nor even the dancing.
It's something quieter.

Spring Mud

I pass another big pickup
covered with thick spring mud
driven by a sober-faced guy in an old baseball cap
sitting next to a big sober-faced dog.

In the truck bed there's barbed wire
and hay leavings and what not,
and up in the back window there's a rifle or two.

It's a comfort to see this man
and his dog and his pickup
because I know that whatever I need
that cowboy will help me with it
for as long as it takes,
and that whatever needs to be done
he can do it.

(Idaho backroads)

Lilies and Children

Faith is the business of mustard seeds,
lilies and children,
the evidence and substance of their being.

Lilies and seeds and children
know to trust completely.
I dare not.
It seems a risky business.

And yet in the evening,
the breeze heavy with blossoms,
the moon a narrow crescent in the west,
and all the world sweet,
so sweet,

I feel a camaraderie with mustard seeds
and a kinship to lilies and children.

Idaho Summer

He promised me a ranch
if I wouldn't go back to Berkeley.
I thought about it.
I thought about fly fishing in Box Canyon,
and the summer nights at the rodeo
when he rode the bucking horses.
I sat on the rail by the chute in the warm dust.

I remembered the hot afternoons in Ketchum,
and the aching smell of the poplars,
and that ranch sounded pretty good.

I remembered the long, soft desert nights
sitting on the tailgate of his pickup,
talking about you and Berkeley.
He hated it that you spoke French.

That was a long time ago.
And after all, you and I ended up in Idaho
to raise the kids.
He bought a ranch.
We lived on the river.

I think about him now and then in the summer
when they rodeo,
and when I take the canoe down to Box Canyon,
and remember the curious way cold water
feels through hip waders.

That was a long time ago.
He's dying now,
and you never speak French.

But the smell of poplars on a hot day
hasn't changed at all.
And the clear spring-water still sings its way
out of the canyon.

The Meadowlark

Please praise whoever made the meadowlark,
set him on a fencepost and taught him
the warble of joy.

"I sing the joy of simple things,
constant things,
gladsome things.
I sing the joy of field and meadow,
willow and poplar,
innocent things.
I sing the pure in heart."

Please praise whoever fashioned feathers
in jaunty yellow hues
to sing out songs of morning through the field.

"I sing the joy of springtime things,
cloudless things,
endless things.
I sing the pure in heart."

Please praise the maker of simple things,
who into bird songs fashioned praise,
and warbles became hymns of grace.

Tuttle Morning

The exuberant sun flows
over the dark canyon wall,
dances in the windows of Tuttle,
sweeps over the roof
to the bright lawns,
then bathes the summer pastures
and settles in the silent desert.

A brilliant morning
of confident goodness.

(Tuttle—my railroad worker shack
above the river at the ranch)

Thinning the Beets

Taking the back road,
I pass six Mexican women in straw hats,
wide-brimmed,
side by side on the ground in the shade of a pickup,
eating lunch.

Behind them is a field of sugar beets.
For them June is sweating in the moist, sandy soil
thinning the young beets.

Rita Morales worked in the beets every June.
She sweat in the hot sun in a wide-brimmed hat
so her children wouldn't have to.

They didn't.

When they visit Idaho
and take a back road,
they pass Mexican women
in straw hats
eating lunch in the shade of a pickup.

Communion

I have no message but can be read
in a homely clump of sagebrush,
no thought so profound as winter,
no hope as articulate as spring.

I have no poem as eloquent
as the thin patch of snow
beneath yellowed Junegrass.

The spirit which quickens
the good and obedient earth
quickens also those who read
the excellent poetry of her integrity.

And there is peace in the communion.

The Poet of Field and Sky

The meadowlark doesn't appear to be trying at all.
He's just sitting on a fence post
singing cheerful heaven's sweetest song.

The genuine is so effortless.

Think you the bit of greatness we all desire
may be the effortless thing
that's ours all the while?

Late Summer Light

Late summer light
drifts through the cornstalks.

Quail scurry by
whistling to babies now grown,
whistling to tasseling corn,

and early autumn's slant of light
that warns of frosty nights

and winter snows.

Down at the River

Down at the river
where quiver slender reeds,
where cattails stand staunchly,
and the red of the blackbird's wing
seems each time more impossibly red,
more exactingly defined,
I see that I have left myself behind.

And I have found the other me by the cattails.
The one that was here before—
too long ago.
But I find, as I always do,
everything is still here.
Everything is the same.

And I, too, am what I became,
but left again and again.

Mid-December in La Honda

I left when the second crop of alfalfa was just ready.
Now the cold desert wind licks the straw stubble
and the brown earth is frozen solid.
Gray velvet field mice huddle in pump houses
and barn walls.

It is nearly Christmas.
The wind flies down long furrows
flattening clumps of pale yellow weeds
and pinning frenzied tumbleweeds against barbed wire,
snapping brittle branches from black elms.

In Idaho the wind blows dry snowflakes
around the motionless legs of mute cattle,
lashing snow against fence posts
and singing telephone wires.

It is mid-December.
Fat green leaves rest against the French window.
The earth is soggy and fecund
and the hills ooze with green life.
Spiders grow fat and slow beneath wet ivy.

I do not know this full and heavy land
with its spawning overgrowth and creeping vines.
I have been too many winters in Idaho,
and some part of me waits for the thin whistle
of the cold desert wind.

(Woodhaven, Santa Cruz Mountains)

Memorial Day

A skinny old cowboy—
faded jeans and high tooled boots—
with a pot of store-bought mums
trudged among the graves.
He'd been there before.
He looked at the little tombstones,
squatted down,
and set the yellow flowers on a flat cement marker.
He's come every Memorial Day
for fifty years,
even though his daughter only lived two days.
He knows she's waiting for him,
and she'll finally get that pony
he wanted her to have.

Morning on Chalk Hill

My matins bore a fruit so fine,
the golden apple of morning was mine.
As it rose above the canyon,
I plucked it with my hand.
I plucked it up and held it,
so round and heavy in my hand.

In the west
the pale round moon was falling to the hill.
I caught it just in time!
And held them both.
I was astounded at my luck!

I stood—I cannot count how long—
bridging sun and moon.
While all around us meadowlarks sang,
"Look, look, look at the hill,
look at Chalk Hill
look at the moon
look at the sun
look at the lady holding the moon
holding the sun and moon."

I held them forever,
just briefly,
until the heavy gold sun rose up
and the thin, transparent moon fell down.

While holding the sun

and holding the moon,
there is no time at all—
only meadowlarks,
and the round and heavy wholeness
in your hand.

Dei Plena Sunt Omnia

The Calendar

I just threw out my old calendar.
Chucked it.

Missed the wastebasket entirely.
It lay there on the floor beneath my desk,
calendaring day after day of holidays and birthdays,
meetings, marriages, dinners, trips and visits,
obligations, business and births.

Day after day of my life looked up at me,
the whole year of delight and distress,
contentment and frustration,
serendipity and dashed hopes
sometimes sharing the same day.

I felt guilty indifferently tossing it all away—
little squares on a calendar page
beneath a painting by Pissarro for December
and Claude Monet for June.

And every single little square complicated
and rich and blessed and difficult and divine.

This year every day is going to be better.
And if it isn't,
and if I chuck the calendar,
tired of the Impressionists,
and miss the wastebasket next January,

every little square will be complicated,
rich, blessed, difficult and divine.

Dei plena sunt omnia.
If all things are full of God,
so our calendar of days is a rich journey,
day by day.

And who can say what day was not hallowed.

Light

If God is light
and God is love,
the divine equation from above
is light equals love.

If energy is mass
and mass the same
and energy light
and love its name,
then all is love,

the essence of God,
not really above,
but here, within, beside, beneath,
God to us did bequeath Himself.

The truer we love
the greater our light
the surer our vision
the clearer our sight.

When our light is constant
and when our love is too,
we'll be as God is,
I and you.

Flying from San Juan to Philadelphia

Were I to have lived only this one day,
this one unremarkable day,
my life would be worth it all.
An uneventful day.
An uneventful flight.
Passengers reading, talking, sleeping.
Flying.
Flying!
Flying through a blinding white cloud world
of stunning and fantastic shapes,
such as had never been
and would never be again.

(Did we not see God?)

An eventless flight.
An unremarkable day.
One like many others.
And each day a priceless pearl
placed on our little necklace,
pearl by pearl by pearl.
And one pearl worth the entire journey.

(Did we not see God?)

I Love Thee Past My Sins

I love thee past my sins,
past my feelings,
and past all things mortal and fallen.

I love thee beyond me.

I love how thou dost make clouds,
and how rain spatters my window,
how wind instantly,
over and over,
remakes the artistry of the sky.

I love how light can drift and flow,
how the sun will come and go,
how puddles shine.

Thou canst make all things plain, radiant.

I love thee past my sins and follies,
past all virtue and striving for the right,
and past utterly all things but thee.

Forgive me that I see thee on occasion only.

Forgive my not taking the offering of thy self
and thus become my own self a crystal drop
of reflected light,

scattering in all directions,
warming all around,
and giving me joy beyond all mortal mischance,
beyond all time,
and all circumstance,
and all suffering.

An offering now too large for my small self.

Grow me, Lord, humble enough,
empty enough
to receive thy large gifts.

Covenant of the Day

Bravely each morning we face our fragile lives,
treading carefully on eggshells,
cautious of what may lie beneath,
concerned with what may be ahead,
judging what is behind.

No exoskeleton to protects us,
thin-skinned and vulnerable we sally forth,
encouraged by flowers and friendly dogs,
simple pleasures and kindly faces.

And by our urgent hope.

Strengthened by the covenant of the day
and steadied by the ordinance of the moon,
we sense that somehow, in some way,
we too are sure and steady and in place.

Secured by the gravity of God.

(Jeremiah 33)

Holiness to the Lord

Abode of Deity,
house of God,
strength of families,
praise and laud
to Him who offers
power to seal—
to bind in heaven
to bind on earth—
evidence of the soul's true worth.
Visions of immortality,
symbols of the perfect whole,
teachings of eternity
flood the thirsting soul.
Immortal realms of Deity
bridged in sacred walls,
His love the strength,
the binding cord.
Holiness to the Lord.

Break of Day

The clouds, a monochrome of gray,
moved at break of day
across a leaden sky.

I watched them,
rather they met my eye,
gray and heavy they drifted by.

Abruptly from the canyon rim,
the sun arose,
the air grew thin,
as crimson, gold, vermilion,
a hundred other hues
infused the clouds with splendor.

Gray possibility at once became
the reflected joy of dawn.

All things bear record of Him whose light
illuminates the soul's dark night,
transforms our muted nature,
awakes our joy in the Son.

The Plain Weave of Wonder

You and I are a divine wonder,
and our ordinary moments are the threads
of the tapestry of each day's elegance and beauty.

Life is not, after all,
year by year, nor even day by day,
but moment by moment.
This moment and now this moment
are the warp and the woof.

Our life is the plain weave of wonder,
the careful cloth of extraordinary moments,
light penetrated,
love infused.

We are like the obscure little blue forget-me-nots,
small and lovely,
and moment by moment never forgotten.

As we weave in tears or joy,
we sit not alone at the loom.

(From an address by Dieter F. Uchtdorf)

Lodestar

I lay on damp grass,
evening damp.
A child then,
looking up at stars
with a wide, accepting look,
comprehending not only stars,
but all mystery.
A child's comprehending,
not of mind, but of union.

The Dipper,
familiar friend,
pointed then,
pointing now,
the Lodestar.

Heavenly guide
point of light
changeless star
through darkest night.
Fixèd point
truth and light
Lodestar, Lodestar
constant, right.

The things of childhood
now are passed—
when did I last lie full-stretch on grass—

and time and change and age distance me
from the child.

But the Lodestar of my soul,
like the Polar Star of night
gives no place to change,
is constant, steady, bright.

(From an address by Gordon B. Hinckley)

The Seed

A tiny black and yellow seed,
lay muddy and cold beneath a weed,
buried many a month ago,
beneath a heavy December snow.

Lifeless, useless, fallen, done,
till April came with April sun.
"Awake!" called Sun, "Thy day is here!"

Gladly Seed the voice did hear,
and rising up with heart so bold,
became a yellow marigold.

That which thou sowest quickeneth not,
nor yet again will yield,
except it die, it becometh not,
flower nor fruitful field.

(1 Corinthians 15:36)

High Places/Narrow Paths

We became as the gods knowing good and evil.
Our privilege to choose, absolute and irrevocable.
Our capacity to choose evil is evident.
Our potential to choose good, limitless.

Sovereign agents of our well-being,
and our misery.

This perilous and splendid enterprise!
This sumptuous undertaking!

None of us are comfortable with it—
we go to high places by narrow paths.

Gifted with grace,
we come out of dark corners into light.

And by doing one wise and kind thing after another,
after another,
after another,
we summit.

And the view is beyond what we could ask or think.

(Genesis 3:22, 2 Nephi 2:27, Ephesians 3:20)

What Think Ye of Christ?

What think ye of Christ?
Wind whispers through poplars,
sun spills in the east windows of Tuttle
on the tremulous call of mourning doves.

Isaiah asks, "Who hath believed our report?"
Light anoints the stillness
and rests on fresh-painted window sills.
The fire snaps, the clock ticks.

What think ye of Christ?
The Savior looks with compassion
on the rich young man
who found eternal life too dear.
I reach out and touch the quiet.

What think ye of Christ?
Thomas Didymus doubted, saw,
and fell to his knees,
"My Lord and my God."

What think ye of Christ?
With Thomas, but without doubt,
wholehearted, absolute, irreversible,
My Lord and my God!

(Meditations from Tuttle, John 20:28)

Strange and Divine Destinies

Salamat (Thank you)

It was in a rain-cooled, narrow bamboo house,
the ornate plastic coffin spanning the small room,
three garish, silver, rented candelabra
affixed to the wall,
and old, blind Leonora lay below them,
stiff and still beneath the plastic viewing glass,
the prayer droning in Tagalog and the eaves dripping.

It was here that I became gently, but completely,
aware that not only was there a Guiding Spirit,
but that all, all that really mattered,
was out of my hands.

My willingness, my availability were required,
but it would seem little else.

And yet more—my desire.

I remembered a poetry class
those long collegiate years ago,
a winter morning of deep snow,
and Edward Taylor's *Huswifery*,
and have often wondered
why the poem stayed with me,
why the line entwined itself,
"Make me, O Lord, thy Spining Wheele compleate."

I was not then "pinkt with
Varnisht Flowers of Paradise."

41

Nor was His "Holy Worde my Distaff."

But the threads were at right angles,
whether I knew it or not.

And day by day, God Himself began to weave,
and to clothe my understanding,
until a decade later, humble and grave,
His ordinances became my fulling mill.

A lifetime later,
in blind, dead Leonora's narrow house
on an island in the Philippine Sea,
I understood fully
the Weaver's control of His wheel.

And I said, Salamat. Salamat, po.

(Linglingay, The Philippines)

Season When Salmon Reach Canyon Streams

Lost in disappearing words,
    words embedded layer upon layer
    with the hope and strength
    and stories of a people.

Stories and words drift and fade
like the transparent strands of still-remembered dreams.

Season When Loaves Are Made from Kouse Root.
    Sun on warm plants taken from the earth,
    roots ground on ancient stones,
    loaves baked by women for hungry children.

Words and stories and wisdom
    blown over the Palouse,
    blown across the mountains of Bear Paw,
    blown like a dream of spotted horses
    into the sun.

Joseph surrendered his rifle, his home, his language.
Can the words be whistled for?
Will they come back again?

If the children learn the language of the elders,
will they learn again who they are?

(Filming a Nez Perce documentary)

Morning at St. Michael's

Sparrows come early to worship at St. Michael's,
the big, empty, pink cathedral
on the road from Gamu.

The birds chatter joyfully, ecstatically,
flitting through the open doors,
stopping for a sip of holy water.

They perch cheerfully on sad-faced saints,
and on yet sadder Marys.
They rest with evident delight
atop the heads of martyrs.

Their religion has a decidedly joyful cast.

The excellent choir swoops and sings
before the bright leaded windows
high above the pulpit,
from which two birds preach
a thoroughly satisfying staccato sermon—
as near as I can tell, on gratitude,

while the morning sun sends rays of glory
through turquoise panes,
and Mary's cadmium blue dress becomes electric.

Sparrow church starts early at St. Michael's.
Soon it will be oppressively hot.

The choir will assume a more hushed reverence
and the congregation will perch quietly
on the backs of the pews,

as sweat drips from the never-changing
faces of the apostles,
and the neon-bright windows dim.

Early morning is the best time for St. Michael's.

Letter from Periche

Let the others sing,
they who have heart for it.
Mine, I wrapped gently
in a new bandana
and gave it to Putama.
Putama,
with whom I have walked
two days in the rain.
Putama,
the prettiest girl
in Namche Bazaar.
To whom I have given
my red flannel shirt.
Let the others dance.
Putama must wait
for her husband of two weeks.
In Namche Bazaar,
in Namche Bazaar,
in Namche Bazaar,
she told me
she was not married.

(From Frank's letter from Everest)

Strange and Divine Destinies

How did I get here—
in this narrow, dark house
on this dark, hot night,
under this dim, bare light bulb
with these thin, dark women
and their thin, quiet children?

What led me to Guibang,
to Linglingay and Upi,
Gawad and Gamu,
and to this gray concrete house
and these earnest-faced women
and their silent children?

My home is across the world.

Why do I love these women and their children
with a love that consumes,
with a love that illuminates dark rooms
and dark nights?

We are all children of strange and divine destinies,
led to our coincidences and our conjunctions,
to our Guibangs and Gamus,

and we find that every child is ours,
and that every path we are led to
leads us to our home.

Offerings in Bali

They say so much,
so softly,
the little palm leaf baskets
of tiny, delicate, blue-petaled flowers,
and still smaller flowers of bright orange,
with rice grains and bits of food
for the gods,
for the ants,
for the birds.

In all the most unlikely places,
a window sill,
beneath a bench,
in the middle of the insane traffic.
Who knows where a god may sup?

Tiny baskets,
sweet and delicate,
common and profound,
wilting in the hot sun.

In the Calm Presence of Death

I was young the first time I encountered death.
It was in Guanajuato in the dark night,
in La Estancia.

There was no electricity.
Dogs howled, a donkey brayed.
A girl said to me,
Come and see my grandmother.
She is dead.
Mi abuelita está muerta.

I wanted to run away,
but I knew that would not respect her grief.
So I went down the dark road,
led by the sound of the chanting and wailing.

Sálvanos, María
Madre de Dios
Sálvanos, María
Madre de Dios

The women were wailing and telling their beads.

Four tall candles burned at the corners of the bed.
I saw the dead woman on her narrow bed,
and I was not afraid.
I thought I would be.

But in the calm presence of death,
I was not afraid.

In the calm presence of death,
there is nothing left to fear.

(From Ellen's letter from La Estancia)

Philippine Moon

The waxing silver moon above Venus belongs in Idaho.
Looking up at the dark sky each night,
I puzzle that it's here in Gamu,
in Isabela,
so far from home,
so misplaced above coconut palms and banana trees.

It belongs above willows, poplars, locusts,
and elms and Russian olives.

Oh, it shows up now and again in California—
superior to competing with freeway lights,
but aware all the same that it's diminished.

But the silver moon's home
has always been the high desert of Idaho,
where it shines undiminished on fields of alfalfa,
and on sagebrush plains,
and reflects resplendently in the river.

Oddly, even the Big Dipper came to Gamu!
That was a shock!

I've come to accept the nightly presence
of the visiting moon,
but I will be glad to take it home with me come spring.

San Bartolomé Jocotenango

The night mists blow through the empty church.
They swirl the dust by the pila of brown water
and whisper down the narrow path
to the silent burying field of whitewashed mounds.
A dog barks.
A flute sounds.

Bartolomé de las Casas came here from Spain.
We walked from the dirt road nine miles away.
They say he built the empty church.
We made a bed of fresh-cut pine boughs.

The church walls are two feet thick.
Birds fly in and out of the glassless windows.

Many years ago I was in San Bartolo,
living in a one-room adobe with no windows,
boiling black beans in brown water.

Tell me, what is it like now?
Tell me, is there a road to San Bartolo?

(Guatemala)

The Mission

It would be worth it all for the cool silence
of clean tile under bare feet,
for the invocation of towering clouds
above flowing fields of rice,
quiet clouds abruptly full of violent rain
blown by terrible winds,

and for the benediction of the children,
children whose sweetness defies utterance,
whose future is at the mercy of hope.

It would be worth it all
for mornings of Dutch chocolate,
and warm bread from a sweltering kitchen
on a street in Gamu,

and studying and talking of things that matter,
of things that matter most,
of the quintessential, the primary, the true,

and the shedding of self to become them.

Then out into the implacable heat
to translate intent into the work
of tender mercies and loving-kindness.

The effort falls short everywhere,
the gap between resolve and result is all too wide,
but the worth of the experience

has become incalculable.

Compelled by quick smiles of grace and beauty,
and the gray, relentless poverty,
we see a sacred blueprint, meticulously drafted,
inevitably unrolling.

Led by divine instruction—
readily available, easily declined—
we work and wonder and sweat in the merciless heat,
relishing the cool, clean tile,
and the excellent thing that has happened to us.

(Serving a mission for The Church of Jesus Christ of
Latter-day Saints)

Lunch on the Ditch Bank

A Bug and I

A bug and I rock together
on the white wooden swing
in the warm September sun.

He's a handsome fellow
with angular legs and graceful antennae.

Looking at him,
I come to understand our kinship,
though he appears to be
a good deal more sound than I,
more confident and self-assured.
And on top of that,
he can fly!

Handsome, focused, confident,
and he can fly.

How little a matter,
how small a bug,
can humble us!

Who Can Be Unmoved?

Who can be unmoved by someone who puts
that particular color of blue on a robin's egg?
Or for that matter, who paints the sky blue
and turns it pink and orange at evening,
and makes the river glisten silver in the morning sun,
and puts songs in birds,

who fills a blossoming and honey-scented tree
with a splendid choir of bees,
and designs high hedges of yellow roses,
and tiny hidden flowers underfoot?

There seems no end to the love of beauty,
the joy of color and sound, texture and light.

I wonder at the faith of those who credit chance.
There seems a designing hand,
and one not unfamiliar with our similar tastes
and shared delight in beauty.

While I'm at it,
the sweetness and orangeness of a good orange,
a warm apple off a late summer tree,
the smell of tasseling corn,
smooth rocks, brindled cats, cheerful dogs.
Where would it stop?

Thank the Designer!
He doesn't need the gratitude.
We do.

November

There's a poem: November.
Word weighted with muted splendor.
November.

Word full of peaceful, pale fields,
and rows of hard yellow stubble,
beneath blue and cloudless skies.
And the sun turned down
to just the right temperature.

Word of fallen leaves,
and of determined still-green trees.
Word full of summer behind,
and snapping fires ahead.

Word full of heavy-laden tables,
and family around them.

November.
Autumn's poignancy nearly over,
winter's austerity yet ahead.

Peaceful, resting, pale November.

The Gnat

I want us not in dark and midnight hours
to lose conviction in our recuperative powers.
They are greater than we think.

I know that from rescuing a gnat
that fell into my sink,
and down the drain,
and looked as if gnat would never be seen again.

Curious, I removed the metal device from the pipe.
No gnat.
Then carefully with tissue into dark hole,
I swept the sides
and rescued him,
or her.

Flattened
stuck
wet
imprisoned on the tissue,
she issued forth,
seemingly as dead as gnat could be.

But still I was curious to see
just how strong a bug can be.
Fragile almost beyond description,
transparent nearly,
delicate and fine,
and apparently finished.

But I worked gently with warm air and hair dryer.
I lifted her finally off the tissue.
I breathed on her.
I watched.

She moved!
Moved on her own!
Alive!
This thing almost too small to see
housed somewhere a strength of life,
in form too frail to fathom,
the power to recover from crippling fate.
The power to be drowned and plastered,
and for no short time,
and to breathe.
And, to my delight, to leave.
She was gone from the counter this morning.

I take from that this lesson:
There must be virtually nothing
our bodies cannot conquer.
They are designed to heal.
And yet my gnat had almost body none.
But with her brave spirit
and fragile frame working as one,
she flew.

If for gnat God did such power endue,
what of me and you?

The Starling

I saw him there,
a skinny, cocky young starling,
perched on the half-opened door
of a country mailbox.

My, he was full of himself!
He looked as if he had just posted
his cheeky letter
to a starling-smitten world.

How does one get to be that confident?
Is it all about flying?

Ordinary People

Ordinary people
aren't.
They don't exist.
Not one.
There's no ordinary story,
where there's birth
there's glory—
heaven's our backstory!
Just look and you'll know
life's a terrific show.
Full of loss and gain,
joy and pain,
sunshine and rain,
and people.
People!
Totally extraordinary,
over-the-top,
and no ordinary people.
Each equipped with a soul,
and the worth of the soul
fills the whole bowl—
running over, splashing, bubbling,
rushing, shining, singing!

Nothing ordinary about that.

Haiku

A black crow eyed me
insolently–and he so
poorly dressed for spring!

Yellow!

Yellow!
Happy fellow to warm my heart, dispel my fears!
Thou great dispenser of daffodil-courage
and dandelion-hope.
Cheering the very dust into a sunbeam!
Proper color of the benevolent sun,
the warbling lark, the tossing wheat.
Spring's earliest herald,
autumn's richest crown.
There's a majesty to red,
the sky is true to blue,
but Yellow, cheerful Yellow,
dear fellow, I choose you!

I Sing the Computer Electric

I sing the computer electric
and praise all things technic
and consider cyberspace
a good place.

Here and there it's run amok
that's our bad luck
with most good things—
the devil has his day—

but I don't go there
so for me
you see
technically
it's all good.

I love the perks
how fast it works
how friendly
how democratic
how cheap.

And how astonishing that anybody can figure it out!
In little mites
of bytes
in pairs of 8
that's how we communicate.

It's so spanking new
so never old
so always changing
so brave and bold

with languages like
Self and Scheme
and JavaScript
Lucid, Perl, and Python
memory by RAM and ROM
and don't forget Oberon.

And the future?
Well, the sky's the limit.

From sequencing genomes
to emailing your aunt
I don't think there're many things
the computer can't
do.

What frontiers!
What vistas!
What peaks!

Let's sing the computer electric
and tip our hat to geeks!

Woodrats and I

Woodrats and I share a love of interior design.
We like to decorate.
I personally like a simple cottage style.
They don't.
They like a brighter, shinier look.
Frankly, I find it too glitzy, even cheap.

Without considering the courtesy of asking permission,
woodrats built a large complex in the old shed
by the locust grove.
I had no idea they had done this.

The work was not without merit.
They used attractive branches and leaves,
some flowers, but the pièce de résistance—
and heaven knows how long it took them—
was gathering up from every part of the shed
all the Mason jar rings and lids,
and weaving them amongst the leaves.

It was managed well, and the effect was good.
What they found, by serious industry, I imagine,
of odds and ends of shiny Christmas pieces
was used particularly well.
Brassy, glitzy, yes, but nice.

I didn't take a lesson from their materials,
but from their eye, their industry,
their persistence, I did.

I puzzled briefly over who owned the lot.
I believe they did.
But as often happens
in unscrupulous real estate deals,
the innocent party is evicted.

I was ruthless,
but not without sincere sorrow for their loss.

Deep Within the Snowy Meadow

Deep within the snowy meadow
underneath the starry sky
lived a little snowshoe rabbit
in his home all snug and dry.

Came the eve of Christmas glory,
Bunny ventured from his nest.
He and all the shining meadow
in a coat of white were dressed.

Quiet was the snowy night
every living sound had ceased.
The little hare in deepest wonder
watched a star rise in the east.

Bunny whispered to his family,
"Come and sit beside me here.
All my instincts tell me clearly
this night we have naught to fear."

Up they came with cautious tread.
How bright the snow seemed to their eyes!
Then to the east they looked each one
and very great was their surprise.

High above and to the east
light of star did increase
till all the meadowland was bright
as snowy diamonds caught the light.

Then saw the bunnies far and wide
across the dazzling meadowside
every beast which they did know,
some were friend but most were foe.

Enraptured by the starry sky
every hostile thought laid by
bathed in radiance from above
they felt the kindly spirit of love.

Now every forest creature knew
the star that rose in velvet blue
foretold a time when fear would cease
and each would dwell with each in peace.

Thus shall it be in ages hence
in meadow, plain, and forest dense
when lion shall lie down with lamb
to honor Him, the great I Am.

The Dialogue

A little boy in a baseball cap
a bluebird
a cheerful dog
and now we have a dialogue
of things great
and of things small
of things that matter most
of things that matter not at all.

An old wood fence to lean on
a bright blue sky to dream on.
Ah, that was the day you knew
the bluebird sang for you.

That was the day the field of blue
went round the world
to Kathmandu
and off again to Timbuktu.

The bird, the boy, the happy dog,
the limitless, unhindered dialogue.

(Debbie's painting)

Summer Lunch

Green frog cooling 'neath thick green weeds,
brown ditch running giving water to the seeds.
Hot sun shining in a pale blue sky,
little bitty moth goes afluttering by.

Deep dusty road under little brown feet,
fat brown sack full of afternoon treat,
juicy red apple and cool green grapes,
thin sugar cookies cut in crescent moon shapes.

Little brown feet into cool brown water,
sit on the weedy bank like Pharaoh's daughter.
Little green frog into water,
kerplop.

Lunch on the ditch bank,
time has stopped.

(Rock Creek, Idaho)

On the Way to My Grandfather's

Grandpa Works Alongside

God and Grandpa share a passion for farming,
for the planting and the harvest.
Both raise excellent alfalfa
and like to watch it drying in the sun,
with its sweet and musty smell of satisfaction.

God and Grandpa have a lot in common.
They both love the morning sun
hitting the ripples of an eddy,
and sun after rain
and pale yellow grain.

God holds things steady.
Grandpa works alongside.

I wonder if it's possible
that God enjoys a pleasant chuckle,
and sometimes laughs outright,
quite cheerfully.

Like Grandpa.

There Were Days of Golden Air

There were days of golden air
golden leaves everywhere
golden moments
brief then
now I can't remember when
it wasn't gold.

The children raked the leaves so high
they touched limbs
touching the sky.
Branches to jump from
and some so high I worried.
But the leaves proved all
required for the fall.

Days so mild
a child could play
till moonlight filled the night
and dappled the grass with shadows.

Below, the river gleamed
and to me it seemed
that if nothing ever changed
if it could be so arranged
I would want for nothing more.

Children's laughter ever after
seems to float beneath the trees
though no one rakes the leaves.

The trees turn gold
the air is soft
but it is lost to us.

We live in populous places
and drive to autumn scenes.
And no one jumps from branches
nor dances round the pungent fire of leaves.
The sheaves of corn are in far fields
and pumpkins sold in stores.

Do the children remember late September
October and November at the ranch
and leaping from a branch
into the colors of autumn?
Do they remember the woodstove,
the fresh apple juice
and the books we read together?

How can what was so utterly alive
be only memories of golden hours?
And if the children don't remember,
what then?

Return Me to the Cloud World

Return me to the cloud world
above the hard earth,
to the peaceful world,
white and soft and invulnerable,

above angles and all edges,
where nothing is brittle,
and sharp cannot exist.

Return me to the unfolding world of white,
a universe of light,
where there can be nothing hard,
no shard
no metal
no hurt
no hate
and nothing is too late.

And whatever fate
wove or spun or cut
that was not soft
is lost.
Vanished.

Where nothing exists
but the white and immaculate world,
the pure and hallowed world
of light.

The Farm

When I was a little girl
I swung on my grandfather's gate
in the hedge of yellow roses.
The hedge sang with sparrows.
From it I watched the cows amble down the lane
lowing to be milked.
At night I slept in the north room.
All night long the frogs sang.
When I am old and have time,
I will try to find my way to my grandfather's.

(Rexburg, Idaho)

Let's Sing the Unsung

Let's sing the unsung—
the exquisite beauty of the gray moth's wing
designed by a master hand.

Let's praise the quiet way she dies,
beneath the light with silent sighs.

Let's honor things humble and small,
things that ask nothing at all.

Leave the world to sing of pomp and show,
let's sing of those who never know
the flash of praise and glory.

Let's sing the humble little moth,
and tell her noiseless story.

A Love Song

Should the time come
when age renders me blank and dumb,
unable to thank you or apologize,
and my oldness tends to monopolize every feeling,
and all that's normal is gone—
words, love, beauty, song,

take now from me what though missing then
will eternally be my love,
and my shame and sorrow
for every difficult hour I cause.

Forgive my blank stare, and if I swear,
and seem not to care.
It is false.
It is not true.
I love you.
I thank you.

And read into the grunts and groans and sighs
these words:
I apologize.
I apologize.

Read into the most vacant stare
what is hidden (who knows where)
these words:
I care.
I care.

Shadow of the Photographer

My mother and her sisters,
all five girls young, pretty, and long ago,
stand together
(high heels, short skirts)
facing the sun,
smiling self-consciously at Grandpa's old camera.

Grandpa's shadow
(My, he was a tall man!)
falls on them.

We all have these captured stories.
This moment is caught,
now this one,
and this.
Save this one!

Life is so fleeting.
All the girls are dead now.
My mother, my aunts.
The pictures remain.

Grandpa's shadow remains.

And stopping the moments,
one after another,
for all time,
nothing lost,
everything saved and stored,

whose is the shadow?

Maybe it's always on us,
covering us as we squint,
self-conscious and half-seeing,
into the sun.

Dad

Old people's lives don't show well.
Those who knew Dad but slightly
often mistook the cover for the book.

At a glance you couldn't tell
Dad's life was crafted with infinite care.
When he got older,
it was harder to see what was really there.

But our lives are handcrafted
and it's all much bigger than we think.
Even when it stops making any sense at all,
and we just sigh and see we're in it for the long haul.

Life is as sacred when there's nothing to it
but getting through it
as at the joyous moments
when the song is in crescendo
and the woodwinds and violins are utterly in tune
and heaven itself would be too soon
and the sound is gorgeous.

Life is no more sacred on that day
than on the one when we lay
confused and quiet
and the song outrageously silent.

It's beyond what we know,

longer than we understand.
And on top of that, handcrafted.

I came to know that when Dad,
old and ill and over,
but for some reason hanging on,
looked at me.

He looked at me
and smiled.

It's sacred.
Big.
Handcrafted.

I tell you what you know.

Tell Me the Way to Cherith

Sleek were the ravens that carried the bread,
the bread and the flesh to Cherith.
Sweet was the water that ran in the brook,
the brook that was called Cherith.
Clear was the voice that came to the Tishbite,
"Hide thyself by Cherith."

Safe was the Tishbite,
safe in the Lord,
fed by the ravens,
he drank from the brook,
safe on the banks of Cherith.

Fed by the birds,
sheltered by God,
cooled by the waters of Cherith.

Please tell me where,
where is the brook,
the brook that runs before Jordan?

Where are the ravens that carried the bread?
Where is the Lord who hid up the Tishbite?

Oh, tell *me* the way to Cherith.

(1 Kings 17)

The Orchard

I lay beneath white blossoms
and watched the breeze make a delicate snow of petals
and heard the languorous murmur of the bees.

This is the poetry
    the drifting hawk
    the secret spider
    the beatific sun.

This is the poem complete,
the wordless explanation of life
in the immutable pattern of being.

Again the sun resurrects the leafless tree
from its winter's death,
again the bee is drawn to the scented blossom.
Nothing is lost.

This is the poem.
This is the simplicity of perfection,
beneath a white tree
lying on new grass
knowing that it is written
immutable
eternal
complete
the poem is written.

(Woodhaven)

Meditations From Tuttle

Language of the Soul

Light is the language of the soul.

October speaks in sentences saturated
in morning mist and evening haze,
in light fragrant with mellow fruit
and dusty harvests.

October speaks a poignant language
of fields of yellow straw
and rivers of reflecting gold.

October light articulates what we can only feel.

What is Art?

What is Art?
Well, that's simple.

It's the voice of light,
the light of language,
the shout behind the whisper,
the whisper behind the shout.

It's the peace of war,
the strength of all things fragile.
The silence of sound,
the sound of silence.

It's the explanation of things
you didn't know you were trying to explain.

The essence of the essential.
The essential thing, whether lovely or plain.
And it's the essence of rain.

Art is the hidden thing
that uncovers the hidden thing,
and discusses it in light and language,
color, form, texture, negative space.

And it's every place.
It uncovers the obvious,
so we can see it.

Almost.

Freeways

Funny how we go to a museum—
sometimes pay good money—
to stand in front of a painting of a pond,
a flower, a portrait of who knows who,
and yet we drive utterly unaware through
or over or under
the genius and majesty and integrity
of the grand colliding of the structural
physical
visual
pragmatic beauty of a concrete cloverleaf,
maybe three of them,
swirling
circling
swooping
ingeniously spilling us off in a dozen directions
through towers and bridges and ramps
of immense strength, power, and beauty.
Funny how much we assume
and how little we sometimes see.

Wood Street CA

People who live on the street
have a shared understanding of the inadequacy
of a blue plastic tarp in a heavy rain
and the lack of protection
in the back of a broken down RV
when it's bitterly cold.

Without water, electricity, toilets
and with virtually no respect from anyone but God,
they live cheek by jowl
in a fantastic collection of the cast-off and unwanted.

They make a life of this, of course,
that's what we do,
but I can only imagine the courage required.
Their sincere gratitude to God takes you by surprise.

People without homes know so much.
They know what rain is and what sun means.
They know how cold cold is and how precious water is.
Like Paul they are instructed how to be hungry
and how to suffer need.

Can I blame them for being a little patronizing
in the face of my ignorance?

(West Oakland)

Khisrow Came to America

Khisrow was a translator for our troops,
ten years in combat.
On the Pakistan border with the 82nd Airborne,
their danger was his.

Khisrow came to America and worked three jobs
so his children would be educated.
"Sameera will be a doctor!
I will send her back to Afghanistan.
They will see what America has done."
Khisrow is a patriot.

Khisrow's wife, Robeena, is learning English.
Her face glows when she says, "See ya later!"

I love this family.
Wholeheartedly.
I go to teach,
I leave having learned.

(Tutoring for No One Left Behind)

The Story

Who you are
tells me who I am,
who we are.

We feel the silver thread connecting us,
fragile and strong and lovely
as a dew-jeweled spider web,

intricately woven from a single source.

Your life is somehow mine,
and mine is yours,
as together we share
this rough and smooth,
sweet and sad,

and ultimately triumphant story.

Training from NYC to Boston

Leafless, frozen Connecticut winter,
under a cold, elongated sunset.

Frozen swamps, frozen ponds.
A crossed-arms tightness to it,
as if relaxing would make it that much colder.
Spare and spartan.

But dressed against it,
I would like to tramp through those woods,
over snapping sticks and branches and dead leaves,
under the bare, cold, patient trees.

And then come home, red-cheeked and virtuous,
to a bowl of chowder,
in that very house,
with the paintless clapboard,
that has weathered a hundred winters,
I think more,

of just such raw and silent days as this.

Gettysburg

Early October,
everywhere.
October in the blue sky,
in the thick, flat grass,
in the turning leaves.

We picnicked on the thick grass.
Tall granite monuments all around us—
Oak Ridge
Little Round Top
Cemetery Hill
Plum Run
Peach Orchard.

All those dead young men.
Dead under a hot July sky.
Dead on the thick grass.
Eight thousand dead in three days.

We picnicked
aware of the blood, dry and gone,
aware of the young men
who looked up at the hot blue sky
and died.

We didn't stay long,
and when we left,
we didn't have much to say.
But Gettysburg went with us.

This Brief Bit of Eternity

I affirm life,
this brief bit of eternity we call mortality.
I know somewhat how painful it can be,
how often it can disappoint,
how thoroughly it tests my good humor.

I would like to say that a splendid fresh morning,
a peaceful sleep,
a pleasant surprise,
the beauty and power of a sunset
spread across the whole of heaven
with color and glory and artistry
beyond our capacity
to even dumbly marvel at sufficiently,

I would like to say that all good things—
sunsets and babies and flowers—
make up for or equal or mask the difficulty
and make it all okay.

But I can't.
I just affirm it anyway.

Life is somehow more important
than whether we like it or not.
We know that.

October Opus

I could roll in the beauty of this wet evening
the way a horse rolls in soft dirt,
rolls all the way over.

I could roll in the saturated colors
the tangible and heavy golds and yellows
and the watercolor sky
just wet enough
to make the grays and blues run together
diffuse and spread across the muted canvas.

And I am in the canvas
in the very opus of October
as the colors and I run together.

Even a difficult day like this
is immaterial
is nothing.

The soft milky air
the yielding, leaf-strewn earth
the opulent light
is more than anything that could happen.

Leaves of Gold, Leaves of Brown

Leaves of gold,
leaves of brown,
falling quickly to the ground.
Autumn passing,
summer gone,
life a brief, sweet-savored song.

What of fear or sorrow ended
when with beauty 'twas well-blended,
and the whole is thus complete,
and the savor rising sweet,
as an offering to heaven,
is the fruit and is the leaven.

Leaves of gold,
leaves of brown,
make for lilies fecund ground.

Passing time but a plaything,
changeless does the rising day bring
intimations full and sweet.
Peace, peace 'tis all complete.

Summer, winter, fall, and spring,
brief melodious songs do sing.
All together an endless whole,
fleeting life, endless soul.

Leaves of gold,

leaves of brown,
falling quickly to the ground.

So all life will quickly go,
like an arrow from a bow.
But the soul all changeless still
does creation's measure fill.

Fall then leaves,
fall and stay.
Time but serves an endless day.

Somewhere Else

Her dying
allowed me to know
that Death,
that big old scary slab of a word,
was just a big old paper dragon.
Why, she didn't die at all!
She just went somewhere else.
And she left behind
all the love necessary.
I miss her—
but time flies.
And I found out that really important thing:
Every tomb is empty.

Singing at the Gate of Heaven

We passed through the remnants of a city
ripped from its foundations by earthquake,
passing the twisted remains of normalcy
where cholera raged.

Haiti once again abandoned
to tragedy, poverty, and disease.

At Foyer de Sion,
at the Gate of Heaven,
we heard the orphans singing,
*Je suis enfant de Dieu, et il m'a mis ici,
il m'a donné un bon foyer, des parents si gentils.**

Little children of God,
singing cheerfully and sweetly
of His love for them,
a love that seemed to saturate the very molecules
of the heavy air drifting around us,

singing of a celestial resilience to circumstance,
a resilience that is Haiti.
A resilience we all share.

(Foyer de Sion orphanage, Port-au-Prince)

*I am a child of God, and he has sent me here,
Has given me an earthly home with parents kind and dear.

Hymns of the Church of Jesus Christ of Latte-day Saints,
301.

Lord, make me equal to my blessings.

DM

Further Acknowledgments

Felix Daggao, Guesno Mardy, and Mary Jeffrey live thousands of miles apart, yet in their uncompromising service, they serve as one. Guesno shepherds orphans in Haiti, Felix guides his flock in Gamu, Mary cares for the homeless and many others in West Oakland. Each serves full-heartedly. They live as if serving others were their bread and their water—an outward sign of inward goodness. They can see life in no other way than to serve.

Nor should we.

It has been my privilege to be inspired and edified by these remarkable individuals and by so many others too numerous to list. These men and women who reach out with love—some rich, some poor, the educated and the pre-literate, the great and the obscure—are great souls, inspiring our respect and lighting our way.

DM